Little Pockets of Glow

Little Pockets of Glow

Poems by

Melinda Coppola

© 2025 Melinda Coppola. All rights reserved.
This material may not be reproduced in any form, published,
reprinted, recorded, performed, broadcast,
rewritten, or redistributed without
the explicit permission of Melinda Coppola.
All such actions are strictly prohibited by law.

Cover design by Shay Culligan
Cover image by Michael Coltman on Unsplash
Author photo by Nick Coppola

ISBN: 978-1-63980-775-8

Kelsay Books
502 South 1040 East, A-119
American Fork, Utah 84003
Kelsaybooks.com

*For my extraordinary daughter,
who will probably never read this book.
I love you forever.*

Acknowledgments

The author wishes to thank the editors of the following books, anthologies, journals and magazines where these poems originally appeared, sometimes in different versions:

Chicken Soup for the Soul: Raising Kids on the Spectrum: "Other People's Children"
Kaleidoscope: "The Way You Show Joy"
Knee Brace Press: "Breaking News About Shoes"
Last Stanza Poetry Journal: "Unbroken," "Honeymoon," "Half Full"
Press 53 anthology: "The Way You Show Joy," "Letting Grow," "Other People's Children"
Songs of Eretz Poetry Review: "Autismville," "The Bus Stop Moms," "Your Repose"
Thimble Literary Magazine: "Nobody"
Vitamin ZZZ: "Night Graces," "Your Repose"
Welcome Home: "Miscarriage"
Willows Wept Review: "Life Cycle of a Day," "Poem to My Young Self"

I also want to thank:

My husband Nick, aka Superguy, for his steadfast love and support.

Dawn Leas, cheerleader, coach and editor extraordinaire.

Victoria Tromara, my dear departed mother who never doubted this book would be born.

My soul sister Marina, who supports me from the Other Side.

My sister moms—too many to name—without you I'd be lost.

Jena Schwartz, Promptress, for a bushel of inspiration and wisdom.

Sue Ann Gleason for her circles, her wisdom, and her generous heart.

My fellow writers from various online groups who provided nourishment along the way

My Yogabilities™ students, for humbling me and widening my perspective.

And to so many, many dedicated teachers, therapists, caregivers, medical professionals, and support staff—your words of encouragement, for her and for me, meant so much. Still do and always will.

Contents

Poem to My Young Self	15
Miscarriage	19
Before Her Beginning	21
Dear November	25
The Room Where Light Meets	27
Expectant	28
Honeymoon	35
Night Graces	36
Mother	37
Walking	38
The Way You Show Joy	42
Turning Point	44
She Who Hears Colors in Songs	46
Nobody	48
7 AM	49
Other People's Children	51
To the Elementary Teacher Who Caused Her Harm	53
The Dance to Spread the Edges	55
Your Repose	56
Shanda	58
Autismville	60
Thank You, Tedium	62
Where Love Resides	65
Light It Up Blue	67
Bus Stop Moms	70
Breaking News About Shoes	73
Who Will Sing?	76
Smile	81
Bridges	83
Father's Day	86
Inheritance	88
Anxiety	90

Harmonious Discord	92
What You Mean	94
Letting Grow	96
My Uncommon Daughter	97
Comfort	100
Released	102
Grocery Shopping	105
The Life Cycle of a Day	108
Unbroken	110
Longing	112
Salt	114
I Must Want This	117
What Not to Do When Decluttering	120
Emergency	123
The Truth About My Slow	125
Perpetuum	128
Waiting	130
My Calling	132
Dear Future Roadmaker	134

Poem to My Young Self

1.
There will be a day trip to New Hampshire
when your family will visit people
you don't remember knowing—
some Albanian community connection.

You'll be standing on a dock looking out
into a moon-sized pond, water like black coffee.
You'll be wearing your sister's wooden Tiki necklace—
so rare she let you borrow anything.

The daughter of these people
you won't remember knowing
will come up behind you,
push you into the obsidian chill.

You'll be scared,
partly because you didn't expect this
partly because you're afraid the necklace will be ruined
and your sister will be so mad at you.

You'll surface quickly,
look to the girl who pushed you
waiting for an apology, an explanation.

Her eyes tilt upwards,
dark almonds inside thick lids,
and her tongue
doesn't fit in her mouth.

She grunts
as she's whisked away by her mother.
Don't be frightened, Love.
Be kind, be ever so kind.

Two years later when you're ten
you'll learn she choked to death
on a piece of meat.
She looked so young, yet you'll never find out
how old she was when she died.

In Middle School
when you finally learn
about Down Syndrome
you'll think of how she pushed you,
how she died.

2.
The boy in your sophomore homeroom—
the one with thick glasses and a lisp
whose shirt is always untucked—
pay attention to your peers parroting

his faltering speech,
the cruel jokes about popular Kim
wanting to be his girlfriend.

Notice the science teacher
barely biting her lip
before smirking along with it all.

Don't be wary, don't go along with others.
Be kind, be ever so kind.

You'll think about him in your mid-life,
when your heart is wider, wiser.
He'll matter to you
in a way your teen-age self
never would have imagined.

3.
You'll realize when you're eight,
remember when you're twelve,
accept when you're sixteen—
your skin feels like it doesn't fit

except when you're out in the woods
with the fairies and the elves,
tending your moss garden.

In your whole long life
you will meet so many others
who also feel misfit—
that third best friend, the first long-love—

and so many more who make it a point
to mock them—
peers and parents,
siblings, magazines telling you all how to look
and speak
and live.

Listen, watch, don't close down.
Be kind, be ever so kind.

4.
You'll say you don't want kids
but someday one will arrive
and she won't fit, won't fit anywhere,

and when she can finally
make herself understood
with flapping hands and grimaces,
and later, with words,

you'll learn her skin
feels all wrong on her,
and most sounds
except your voice
have always been too loud.

You'll be her interpreter
and when people ask how to be with her
you'll tell them—

Don't be scared.
Don't look away.
Don't talk about her
as if she isn't there.

Be kind. Be ever so kind.

Miscarriage

And now this aching,
arms circling the dry space
your absence leaves, cold hollow
in the base of my spine as if I'd expanded
bigger than you ever were
to mourn you,
empty swollen womb a testament to my
yearning and my sorrow, an internal
gravestone for my flowering grievings.

You were never mine.
I never held your vernix-covered head
against my chest, my rhythmic heart
an explosion of joy, an invitation
for praise. I never heard your staccato
music break the air, first breath
released in primal exhalation.

My glance never embraced
your tiny form, never committed
to memory that first contact—
eye to amazed eye—
as we tumbled headlong into our lifetime
of adventure, nurture, love.

Sweet Nameless One, there is a space
pressed in my heart for you, a capsule
of sacred air that bears your traces,
a blank journal,
(yes, a whole one, not just a page)
I've tucked into my collection
to commemorate you.

The universe has its reasons.
I hardly know how I continue.
Cyclic ebb and flow,
quest for new growth, your brief
traces fertilizing the landscape of my sorrows.

Before Her Beginning

There were desert years—
waiting out treatment
for the stabbing pain of endometriosis,
cycles suppressed by pills.

Physical agony faded
as I hyper-focused on pregnant bellies
on the streets, in stores,
blossoming from the midriffs of friends.
My heart grew sore with wanting.

My thirtieth birthday loomed—
doctors gave the green light—
Not much time, don't wait.

Hope came in waves, crested
then dropped each month
with the arrival of that scarlet flag
signaling *no, not now, not yet.*

Anxiety was a headlight
casting shadows
that appeared longer
in the rearview as each month
came and went,
as my womb remained uninhabited.

There were the trial years—
pills, shots and imaging,
thermometers and charting.

Every floor in the little place
I shared with my husband
felt spackled with eggshells.

He'd meet me at the fertility clinic,
make his contribution in a closet-like room,
hand a tube to some young nurse
before running off to grad school.

After a few minutes
they'd hand me a precious vial
of spun-down supersperm
and I'd drop it
between my breasts
to keep it warm,
grab a subway across town
to the crusty, old GYN's office.

I'd lie on the metal table,
lower half shivering,
sandwiched between paper sheets.
Praying he'd hurry in
as those little sperm lay dying
in their vial.

Finally, a gruff hello.
Gloved hands clumsy
with the cold speculum,
he'd inject that vial deep
into my hormone-addled uterus.
I'd head off to my desk job
cramping and hoping.

There were the three starts—
when pin-sized zygotes
cleaved to my crimson insides—
Elation! Cells divided
into pink pearlescent buds.

My warm nest grew purposeful, plush
each time those sprouts became embryos
tapping out cardiac rhythms.
My triumph got fat on expectation

but like disgruntled guests
that found my accommodations lacking
those rootlets never stayed too long.

More ultrasounds.
No heartbeats.
I'm sorry. This happens. Keep trying.

I was spent, despondent and always cold,
ready to accept defeat
that dreary March when she arrived
from some distant star
and planted herself deep inside me.

She settled in
and didn't leave
until the wee hours
of a frigid November night
when her perfect pink head
cracked me open,
heart and all,
and I have never been the same.

Afterwards, once the Universe
had dispatched this rare creature to me, to us,
two more seedlings over
two more years
tried to root inside me,
found the soil lacking,
left.

This is my story,
by which I mean
my sacred God-winked parable.
How else can I explain
her arrival, or the gospel
of gifted mysteries and trials
she came bearing?

Dear November,

I'm a poet who's having trouble poeming right now. So being amiss, Miss Construed, I'm writing a letter instead.

You are special to me, 11th month, in your own glorious, necrotic, achingly beautiful way. I mean, each page in the book of numbers we call the calendar is rich with grief and pleasure, memories of arrivals and departures, and years of holding on tight while the New England leaves were letting go.

But you hold more in your numbered boxes, 30 in all. More happy, more sad—more than some months combined. Letting go, dear month, is not as easy as the fall flora would have us think.

For starters, one tiny towheaded boy arrived, your 28th day, 1926. Do you remember? He came up amid hardships, I was told, the kind I've never known. He was reared with some violence, it was whispered. His demons followed him, baring fangs in a frightening temper and the discipline he thought best to deliver to children. That I did feel and see echoed in my own book of numbers.

Another November, decades later: One grown woman (that would be me), who thought herself adult, pledged herself to one grown man, whose heart, perhaps, she barely knew. Your 4th day, year 1989. Does that tickle your memory? There was an audience; most attendees were invited, but Fear and Anger and their young wisp of a Sorrow slipped in unasked. Towheaded 1926 dressed up as bald-headed middle age and walked me down the aisle. I matched my step to his. Too fast, but I sped up anyway.

And then 1992, your 15th day, gave us a child. She was not the only pregnancy, just the only one to make it out of me alive. Did you have a hand in that, November? She was perfect, and there was joy. 1926 and 1989 were pleased.

Things got broken along the way. Things often do. 1926 finally learned to let go, and pieces of him became soil, leaf, and flower. 1989 fell hard and cracked wide open. There are scars, but they are tough and fibrous and have served me well as I raise up one fascinating young woman.

She has been, well, sort of *dissed* by this time and place. She is called *dis-abled.* She is *dis-affiliated* with what society calls normal and her very being *dis-allows* anyone else's notion of what she should be. Oh, and a few who claim to love her have so *dis-tanced* themselves from her that they have essentially *dis-appeared.*

She, though, has *dis-assembled* my expectations of motherhood, sometimes in the most delightful ways. She will *dis-abuse* you of your understanding of how words are used, if you let her. She is *dis-arming,* full of surprises and an innocence that shines. She also *dis-tills* my meaning-of-life questions in a way my poems never quite do.

And so, dear November, old friend, you have grown big in my small incarnation. I celebrate you well—the way I wish we all rejoiced when someone dies because we are happy for their soul, because we know they have graduated from the toughest school there is.

I salute and bow down to you for gifting me the ability to love beyond measure, to mourn and wail and clutch grief way too tight. Then to breathe deeply and let go like the leaves you coax to their next fertile phase, the ground growing rich under your sanguine discipline.

Gratefully,
Melinda

The Room Where Light Meets

Perhaps it began in a vast,
cloud-filled room,
backlit with stars
and random flashes
of lightening.

Perhaps it began in the distilled bright
of a hundred thousand dawns
traveling at the speed of light
to meet and coalesce
before The Beginner of All That Is.

Perhaps it began
when we received our assignments.
Days marked
with celestial purple ink
in that ethereal datebook—
your conception,
and birth—
you, a child,
me, a mother.

Perhaps there is no random,
no haphazard,
no accident.

Perhaps we were—
and are—always
right on time.

Expectant

Those hefty volumes
lined up
on the bookstore shelf,
alphabetically by author,

their bright pictures inspired me—
rosy babies,
glowing mamas,
eager dads
and beaming
siblings,

bonding and smiling
as if born for photo opps,
cheerleading procreation.

Breast vs. bottle,
cloth vs. disposable,
space your pregnancies
for maximum joy.

They didn't tell me
about the parade of doctors—
not just pediatricians
but also
neurologists, and gastroenterologists,
psychiatrists and urologists—
all willing and eager
to proclaim what was amiss
with my winsome
sweet-cheeked bundle.

The therapists—
occupational, physical and speech—
the behavior analysts
and lists
and lists
and lists.

Chart target behaviors and peeing—
the whens and how longs
and what happened just before.

Try no dairy
no gluten,
no sugar,
no soy.

Remember to keep track.
Come back in two weeks, a month, or six.

Bring your records,
lists, charts,
and video of that flapping,
those meltdowns.

Could it be seizure?
Come on down,
get your 24-hour sleep-deprived EEG.

Could it be mitochondrial disease?
Step right up for a muscle biopsy
four states away that'll leave
a three-inch scar on her left thigh.

When the results are inconclusive,
here, have a 4-month supply
of expensive mitochondrial cocktails
to force down her throat
every morning.

Nothing in those books
told me that the words
tacked on to my child—
autism
obsessive-compulsive disorder,
lordosis,
anxiety disorder,
kyphosis,
polyuria,
hypotonia
circadian rhythm disorder—
had a silver lining.

They got her services,
which, at first, I thought
might Fix Everything.

Those books, picture-perfect,
never foretold school-year scenes
of the teacher who terrorized her,
the one I learned years later
dragged her across the room,

or the OT who called me at home
rather late at night
to tell me she felt threatened
by some words
my girl scribbled
in her private journal,
and there would be an emergency
team meeting to discuss it.

The conferences
when she'd been vomiting daily
for weeks from some sheer terror
she could not communicate.

She wasn't using the right words—
the ones they could understand—
or any words,
wasn't able to quell her compulsion
to touch other people's noses.

She bit one teacher so hard
it left a purple bruise.

Fifteen years later
she found the language to tell me
the three words that teacher
said that day—
"I hate you."

All the objectives
designed by professionals
to normalize and quell behaviors.

Years of goals
that I wanted to mean everything,
but ended up meaning very little.

No hint, in those hefty volumes,
that my child could trek
through 20 years of school
without ever having a real friend.

There are no shiny photos
of me, immune
to menstrual blood
and poop on the toilet seat,

of me, on my knees
tubside, shampooing
my adult daughter's hair,

of me, in the kitchen
packing lunch,
showing my 28-year-old
how to apply Chapstick
for the hundredth time.

Driving her here.
Driving her there.
Never, ever leaving her alone.

They didn't warn me
the first adult-day program
wouldn't, in fact,
take her out frequently
as promised,
or let her cook in that nice big kitchen,

or respond to her
mostly, or at all,
as she practiced self-advocacy,
which was her goal.

The second day program
wasn't pleased
with those pee accidents,
nor would they deign
to interpret her private language
to know when she's broadcasting distress.
No one told me
she'd need me night and day,
that I'll love her
more than I knew possible,
sometimes more than I can bear.

But damn! I get tired.
The kind of wrung out that
causes looks of concern
when I meet up with friends.

They didn't even hint,
those shiny books,
that her father
might give up on our marriage,
and, later, on her too,

as if she never brought him joy,
as if he doesn't have a daughter
who lives just a few towns away.

Those childbearing bibles
will never begin to explain
what it feels like
to watch nieces and nephews
graduate, go off to college,
move into their adult lives.

How heavy
it is to look at my own mortality
and her vulnerability
and try my darndest
to be positive, upbeat, unafraid.

There is much darkness on this road.
It makes the lights, when they appear,
seem so bright and beautiful.

My own dark is chock full of luminosities,
little pockets of glow.

Honeymoon

In Kenya, on the plains,
armies of fine golden dust
rose and swarmed to every living thing,
clung to skin and lips,
tongue and cornea,
the camera's shuttered eye.

Who can say when a marriage begins or ends?
There are no dreams here
she might've thought, *no poems.*
At night, under the mosquito netting,
perhaps she watched his back rise and fall,
didn't sleep but mourned
the years ahead.

Three decades later she excavated
a brown book of photos, met
a man and a woman, young and familiar,
hats angled away from the dust or each other.
Against a backdrop of zebras grazing,
with elephants walking in the distance,
the two squinted straight into the camera,
the swirl of dust already coming between them.

Night Graces

Each sleep cycle you wake happy,
chirping psalm-songs into the darkness,
warm circles of air
rising from your curled body.

You tumble toward my bed,
proclaim morning
whether it is midnight or three
or more thankfully, five,

and I surface
from moon dreams
to embrace you—
little Talitha of Ursa Major,
Gemma of Corona Borealis—

insistent beacon,
nudging my fatigue aside
so this perfect view of the stars—
glorious jewels of the night—
reveals itself as the gift it is

and I, your student, humbly bring you
a glass of water.

Mother

You wake in the middle of the night.
This is not new. I move
dreamlike to your bed, empty my pockets,
open my arms, offer water and all
that which is music for you—soothing words,
the moon time sway of murmured
song and dance, our odd routine.

Someone lost her only child tonight,
tightened her grasp around
small bones, soft skin still warm,
closing those tiny eyes
in a final gesture of care-taking,
shielding her baby
from her own wracking grief
or a last view
of their world of
famine, war, desperate pain.

Two continents away we feel the shudder,
and I squeeze you a bit too hard,
almost knowing why,
and millions of us everywhere
do this dance night after night,

reaching and holding and rocking,
wiping the same tears.

We are all one mother,
loving and nursing
and mourning
the same beloved child.

Walking

At twelve, thirteen,
fourteen months,
when most children
begin to walk,
or make a show
of pulling their soft
wobbly bodies
to stand,

you were content
to sit and rub
the carpet, watch
the fibers grow fuzz
beneath hands
you didn't seem to know
belonged to you.

A plump child you were,
with flesh-ringed legs
and arms,
at least three chins.

As you grew
stronger, my arms
did, too,
carrying you
room to room,
holding you
while you screamed
inconsolably

and turned away
from family and friends
who reached out
hoping for a smile, a cuddle.

You recoiled
at some sights and sounds,
textures, certain clothes,
and any kind of shoe.

We didn't know about autism,
not yet,
but I quickly learned
what brought you comfort—
chirpy music, breastfeeding,
being driven in the car
for hours.

When you were at peace
I could be, too.

I wonder
if you recall,
as I do,
when you were sixteen, eighteen,
twenty months
plopped on the grass,

making a study,
it seemed,
of the individual green blades,
your fat hands
brushing the tops of them
over and over,
your face a mix
of stern concentration
and happy fascination,

sweet reprieve from the screaming,
relief for my strong
but tired arms.

And still you grew,
rebuffing my attempts
to hold you up by the armpits,
sing walking songs,
show you videos
of babies toddling happily
from toy to toy.

It was the not walking
that brought my questions
to doctors,
to Early Intervention,
to a parade
of specialists and therapies
I never dreamed
would become our norm.

That time was a blur
in many ways,
but I recall
your first,
tentative steps.

You were two
years two months,
finally ready
to trust your feet
against the hardness of the earth,

to step forward
into the blur
of delight and confusion
newness and noise.

The Way You Show Joy

Your smile dips in the middle,
then gains momentum, pushes wider
as if your cheeks will burst
with strain. But they continue
upwards
into little moon hills, gentle rises
in front of your eyes, your hands
gyrating high in the air.

Small voice sweet on the eardrum,
A patchwork of symphonies—
Green girls in kitchen passed away,
panda we will go Madagascar
eating peaches on the beach—
a birdy, surprised song
in answer to everything.
You love words unconditionally,
without comprehension, for their sounds alone.

In a restaurant, in line.
Stay close to Mommy. Quiet hands.
There is no touching people we don't know.

Nearby a man sits over his hamburger,
unaware of the siren song his bald, shiny head
broadcasts. Your quick hands dart out
to tap, tap, tap, as if bestowing forgiveness.
He turns sharply, meets my apologetic smile, nods.

Your exuberance shakes me from my worry,
which is my doom.

You navigate this unpredictable world
with little to lean on except me.
I can interpret the actions of the aliens,
fluent as I am in their ways.

We're co-authoring a book we'll call
The Strangers Guide to the Strange.
Touch these but not those, unless home.
Not too close, hands down.
Use this word now, watch people's faces.

If angry, their eyes will squish down,
mouth will be straight.
If happy, they will make big cheeks and smile.
OK for you to smile, too.

Dark is for sleep.
If you say the same thing over and over
it becomes boring.
People don't like to be licked.

Your horizon a rolling sea,
you cling to me for safety—
yet that smile for a blue-sky day,
your oversized delight
in wind among grasses—

What deft spirit drizzled this
autism into your essence, or did
you choose it before you were born?

Turning Point

It was a gradual thing—
two people turning inward,
shifting away from
the other's eyes,
two bodies of skin
growing used to
not touching each other.

My heart ached
as it turned from a sweet, pliable grape
that was now pruning,
now turning brittle,
shelled, hard.

I do remember
the exact moment
my heart cracked open—

my miseries,
nights alone beside you,
my cries for your ears,
your eyes, your
tenderness,
all my fears,

all burst forth
into my body
like a hundred tiny shards
of glass.

I'd been begging again—
please talk to me,
please listen to me
please love me—

and you barely turned
from the computer screen,
grabbed my right wrist
with your left hand,
twisted hard
as your voice
floated somewhere above my head
saying

I want my life back,
I want my life back.

She Who Hears Colors in Songs

A collection of can'ts, never wills
and less thans. A bucket of myriad ways
she comes up short.
Autism.

The rusty scuttle
whose name expands
to encompass
the others—
Obsessive Compulsive Disorder
Severe anxiety disorder.
Chronic polyuria.
Lordosis, Kyphosis.
Intellectual Disability.

Oh, I've made peace
with all the labels,
pocketed them, even,
as keys to the kingdom
of Getting Services.

The real of our story
lives behind that big bucket,
told and retold
at home, in the car,
on our daily walks,
woven into all our routines.

Worry for her safety
and future looms large,
and for that alone,
this wish to stay alive
as long as she,
well past my allotted time.

Yet sure as sunrise,
deep as canyon,
boundless as evening sky
lives certitude—
my daughter knows
her names:
Love.
Loved.
Beloved.
She Who Hears Colors in Songs.

And her other names,
also true,
which she may or may not
recognize—

Patience Coach.
Systemizer Extraordinaire.
Incognizant Teacher
of the Core Curriculum of the Heart.

Nobody

Hours at your computer
behind a closed door,
and I lived like a widow,
mothered a fatherless child,
respected your choice
to close up tighter and tighter
until you seemed to cease
being there at all.

Your home office was a ship
that broke free from the house
and sailed off into scholarly oblivion.

Back on land, grappling
with our child's diagnosis—
lifelong, they said. No cure—
my heart twisted itself into knots,
bled and scabbed and bled some more.

I surely felt enough for both of us.
My thighs, buttocks, arms
expanded so I could be two
parents and I bravely carried on—
all smiles for the camera,
parroting hope
with feigned tranquility.

Nobody but me
knew you were gone.
Nobody noticed the vacant space
that gaped between us.
Nobody knew just the moment
I stopped watching
for your return.

7 AM

I entered your room quietly,
with loving stealth,
stood inches from where you curled
into the warmth of your sleep nest,

pausing one round moment
to take in the sight of you,
to hug you with my eyes
before we began
the ritual we'd perfected
over two decades of mornings.

There we were in our assigned places,
me leaning gently above,
you just beginning to stir
as I sang you awake.

There were your hands
reaching for my hair,
first right side, then left,
like a touchstone
to remind you it's safe
to be awake and alive.

Pink walls and ceiling, pastel rug,
whispered, made-up song,
you under assorted spreads,
a quilt, some blankets,

one embroidered with your name
and the date you debuted,
a gift from a relative
on your absent dad's side,
whose name I've quite forgotten,
who is surely long dead.

I flash-mused on what she'd feel,
this nameless giver of named blankets,
if she could ghost unseen
into your bedroom, this morning
to see what you've become.

Would it be grief
for all the ways you'll never be,
diagnoses not yet named,
a baby who would remain,
in many ways, a child?

Would it be curiosity?
Your perspective
tapping on the doors
of her phantom compassion,
awakening a deep patience,
a human reunion with her own
estranged otherness?

I hope she would be filled
with the color of pure delight
as she saw you still loving
her decades-old gift,
for its essential pinkness,
its enduring softness,
its well-named comfort.

You dream here
in the place you call safe
where you are perfect
with no one there
to tell you otherwise.

Other People's Children

I am different, not less.
—Temple Grandin

It's the little ones who unnerve me.

They seem to leap to the top of the jungle gym,
swinging by one hand, they jump
and land on two feet, laughing.

Their words weave simultaneously
stories, negotiations, insults,
laughter and shrieks of shared delight.

They size each other up:
the bully, the smart one, the prima donna.
Roles that shape them for the rest of their lives.

Around the perimeter of that same play yard
you stride, little alien, measuring
the meters with the rulers of your legs.

Your gaze is on the treetops, where leaves
dance in the air and speak a fascinating language
only you can hear.

You stop to fling your hands
wide, first one and then the other,
flicking your fingers quickly in a rhythm
that must soothe your ruffled senses.

In a world where making sense means making cents
the children on the play yard,
other people's children, are already matriculating,

and you don't even know
you're left in the dust, and if you did
you would have only odd delight—

The way fine dirt particles shimmer
in the translucent air. The way the leaves
dance to meet your frantic fingers.

To the Elementary Teacher Who Caused Her Harm

I like to think
I don't hold grudges,

being a teacher
of presence and compassion.
I do practice
seeing the light
in everyone.

I like to think,
but feeling is a different window.
It illuminates rooms
of my daughter's past,

in which I can't help.
I watch in horror
scenes of you
hurting her—
verbally
physically
emotionally—

playing and replaying
through the chambers
of my heart, devastation
bouncing off the soft pink walls,

creating and sustaining
a kind of wailing,
a keening
for the chunk of innocence
you stole from her.

I didn't know. She couldn't tell.
The only proof,
her guileless retelling,
now that she can,
including dates and times.

My daughter is incapable of lying.

Could I have known?
This will always haunt me.
I read books and articles,
listen to audios
telling me how to clear space
in my house

my mind
my body
my soul—
which is my true home—

and I long to erase you
from my being and from hers.

OK, that's not the truth.
Erasure sounds gentle, careful.

I really long to burn you
from memory,
would gladly sear my flesh and even hers,
then cauterize

and let the healing
at last begin.

The Dance to Spread the Edges

Not much for dancing
I'm more of a plodder,
a trudger, a dilly dally-er.

My heart, however, wears tutus,
goes all *en pointe*
if you give me

a song, a tree, a sunrise,
another glorious day
to traipse through.

Give me the gift of my daughter
with all her autisms showing,
and I'll hum my way
to the very edges of my skin.

My love will keep spreading
so it oozes through my pores
and fills rooms,
a whole town, an island, even.

My outrageous tenderness
will rainbow
the hell out of
any slab of silence,
airborne or not.

Give me slack here,
I'm telling you
this is how I dance.

Your Repose

When the eyes dance
beneath closed lids,
the dream stage known as REM,
is also paradoxical sleep,
because the mind is quite awake
while the body is resting.

I wonder if your soul
checks herself in mirrors
as you slumber, scrolls
Facebook, idly clicking "likes"
with her ethereal fingers,
as if the flick of a mouse,
could change a life's course.

You walk the waking world
following all the rules you know,
making up some you don't,
doing everything in order,
trying to make sense of the chaos.

You who count duplicates;
numbers on license plates,
yellow cars in a lot,
who checks and rechecks
the solid fences of her world—
I will have a treat,
You're a girl,
You will have girl hair when we leave.
No bun, hair down.
Touch nose to cheek.

Mommy can you fix it?

I want to think you are free in sleep—
that autism and obsessions
can't follow you
when you fly to that misty realm.

I want to think
you can have this respite every night,
relief from all the voices, and fears,
the tensions, demands,

that there is no standard
of normal in dreamland,
or, if there is, you define it,
and rest quite comfortably there.

Shanda

When I was 27 and engaged
to be married, I learned to be a Jew.
Took the course, passed the test. I slipped into
the Mikvah without so much as a ripple,
as if I'd done so monthly for a decade.
The blessings tumbled from my lips.
Behind the door the Rabbi broadcasted pride.

I changed my name for a love
I read about in books,
metamorphosized into someone else's guess
of what a wife should be—
of what his wife should be.
It's a double mitzvah on a Friday night the Rabbi
said slyly, and the conversion class twittered.
The blond, Catholic wife—one half of the couple
next to us—blushed crimson.

Covering my eyes to light candles,
I must have missed some clues.
Don't sing, I know he said, *you are out of tune.*
Out of sync. Out of love.
You are, I think he said,
so uninteresting to me
and later,
I want my life back.

His life or his wife?
If that's what he said then it must be so. Hard.
Must be so hard to live with me, and with the child
we struggled to conceive.

She was as imperfect as her mother,
he may have thought,
flawed in deep and mysterious ways.
That autism must have come from some
maternal thread, some beaded gene.

Ten years on, slowly learning
to sleep again
alone.
I hug knees tight against my chest,
rock maybe an hour this way each night,
ritualizing the seep of body heat
into the sheets,
davening against the darkness
davening into the dream-lit nether land
where he still loves me,
where I look into a mirror
and something pretty looks back.

Note: *Shanda* is a Yiddish word that means shame or disgrace.
Davening, also Yiddish, translates to recitation of prescribed Jewish prayer, often done quietly or silently while moving the lips.

Autismville

It's no unpleasant thing
to live in the quirky neighborhood,
on the far side of the river,
away from the thickest part
of the frantic throng.

Nor will I say it's tragic
in this parallel universe—
peopled with other folks
who understand the need for things
like space and patience
velvet compassion,
smooth voices, soft dolls,
and more spice in everything.

Here, we spend time looking up,
fixating and stimming
on green minnow leaves
that shimmer against the waters of the sky.

Here we have our own customs-
the recitation of dreams,
the pre-breakfast questions
and videotaped answer
to play back over and over.
The reassurances:
Yes, there will be snack. Yes, Mom is a girl.
Yes, Mom will wear hair down when we leave.

The life we've grown into,
first she and I and then he
who married into this confluence
of ordered disorder,
has authentic charm.

We go slow.
We don't try to measure up.
Our victories are sweeter
for how long they take to manifest,
and mysterious
for how quickly they can disappear.

We have magic here, I tell you.
Songs that play in color,
voices with texture,
folks who spin and swing
and hum and sing.

And the leaves!
The glorious minnow leaves!
How happy they look,
dancing upstream
between the clouds
and laughing.

Thank You, Tedium

In the midst of the interminable news—
all-bad-all-the-time,
chaos and tragedy,
aftermath and predictions,

close-ups and sound bites
that feed worry
and starve hope,
invite helplessness

inside this modern quotidian,
there is something else.
Not exactly calm, but steadier ground,

and I, who have recently
allowed *my own heart* to rent space
to darkness and fear,
watched myself mistrust
this solid ground,

guessing it to be the eye
of the larger storm
which I've been naming
How Things Are Now.

This morning, my daughter's needs
rose strong and clear,
as they often do.
I turned my intention
towards her, and then,
felt cool, hard floor beneath my feet,
and there it all was before me
spread out like a map
for my frayed senses:

The morning tea and reading her dream.

A string of reassurances
against her fears of the day.

The mechanics of a smoothie.
First juice then fruit,
now let's shield our faces from the splash
of berries into liquid,
earplugs before blender.

Morning pills and pink shirt, yes.

Let's try the pants again,
this time with the tag in the back,
and oops! Your shoes found the wrong feet.
Can we make those laces nice and tight?

Packed lunch, yes.
the soup is salty,
the pickles tart, yes, yes.

There will be late sleep on Saturday.
Yes, Mom is a girl,
yes we will go out this afternoon,
yes you will have a snack.

and in the thick of our rituals,
a slow, slow dance of repetition,
naming all the parts of the day,

I almost fell to my knees,
silently thanking
God/Goddess/That-Which-Makes-Stuff-Happen,

for the ordinary work of caregiving,
sweet tedium
tethering me to the here and now,
almost sacred in its simplicity.

Eyes on task at hand,
my heart hums

with the love that fuels
this tending.

It binds me
to that which is real and necessary,
lifesaving and true.

Where Love Resides

It's in each morning—
the tiny
flutter in my chest
as I stand before the window
contemplating another day
to play and struggle,

to bear witness to miracles
hiding in plain sight—
the squirrels
finding sustenance
in the deep February freeze,
the way morning ice
clings to the bare trees
like forty carats of sparkle
in the early sun.

It's my daughter's hands
tickling the air
as she reaches for my hair,
and her sweet soprano
giving new life to old songs.

It blossoms like Spring
from my yoga students
as they sink
into deep relaxation,

then rise to sit, open
their eyes to the wonder
of each other,

bowing to the prayer hands
of the one across, next to,
four mats away,

and to me as I take in
the essential goodness
that rises heat-like
from their heads,
casting shimmer halos
just above
their awareness.

It's the pure beauty
of my cats,
their unself-conscious edict
to me or anyone
with ears to hear,
eyes to see.

Be present, they say.
Just sit and be
content with me.

Light It Up Blue
Autism Awareness Month and World Autism Day

In case the day lacks color,
(as if any day with autism in it could be dull),
the mysterious Namers-of-Days-and-Months
have painted it a medium sort of blue.

I wonder who decided this
and how it was chosen,
this perfectly ordinary second day,
and weighted with a long middle
moniker, like a fish
plucked out of the ocean,

tagged and thrown back
into what used to be
a perfectly ordinary fourth month.
And why a color?
Does autism look like blue
to outsiders?
A sky, a field of lupine
or delphiniums?

Pondering this, I roll up my sleeves,
prep the tub for the one
who turned my life on its ear,

she who makes me laugh,
who wears me out,
who is a master of repetition
and defies reduction,
who is many-hued.

She who is unaware of your awareness,
who, if asked, what you think of her,
would mutter "Not interesting,"

she who needs help with a bath
but can take a thing
and spell it backwards,
report to the air/no one in particular
how many redundant vowels it contains,
and how her lunch reminds her
of *Home on the Range.*

She who hears songs in color,
who does not stay in her bed all night,
who is frightened of beads with holes,

she who knows if there's a day to be aware of
it's the fourth Friday in February,
which she calls Ate Baby Kate, and that means bad,
and therefore must be worried about
many months in advance,

she who can sing whole CDs in order,
who tells me thirty times a day
that I'm a girl (in case I forget)

She who needs more than I have
gives more than I need
has more than you think,
who is more, so much more,
than you give her credit for.

And so, dear you-who-aren't-aware,
please allow me to set the record straight.

Autism is multi-colored,
and awareness is every single day,
and no blue second day
of any fourth month
will ever matter more
than your interest,
your kindness, your respect,
your willingness
to help us challenge
a world that would reduce anyone
to an assumption
or a label
in one color
on one day
within one month.

Bus Stop Moms

From my morning window
I watched
as they huddled casually,
tossed light conversation
back and forth,

an occasional
eye towards their kids
who played and laughed
together, tracing shapes and letters
in the dirt with sticks.

After the big, yellow bus
swallowed their chattering children,
the moms stayed and talked
a bit, in the easy way
women do
when they have things in common,
like an intact marriage,
and Pilates class,
and typically developing children.

I watched them wave—
good-bye, see you later—
as they each turned
toward their well-manicured lawns,
highlighted hair shining in the sun.

I guessed at market lists,
soccer schedules,
Girl Scouts tomorrow,
Johnny needs new sneakers—
such busy mom thoughts
dancing in their heads.

From behind a fraying lace curtain
I imagined being one of them.
How carefree they must feel,
sending their kids off
without concern
for their lack of toileting skills,
compulsion to pull braids or pigtails,
inability to communicate.

Without gnawing worry
that today might be the day
she bites the teacher again,
(who tells her to wait for the bathroom),

or rips at her clothes at recess,
(because it's just too loud),

or has a meltdown during snack time,
(because the juice was the wrong color,
and nobody noticed signs
of the impending storm).

Almost two decades later,
the bus-stop moms
are all grown up,
and so am I.

We still live in parallel universes,
they in their emptying nests,
kids off to college,
getting engaged,
traveling the world,

and I rarely compare
my apple to their oranges
these days,
having found the appetite
for what I have been served,

which is another way of saying
we can learn to love
what we've been given.

I'm busy slow dancing
a day, a week at a time,
having found my own
special mom circles,

and a different carefree
that doesn't demand
grades, degrees, weddings,

having found a partner who
loves being her dad.

Different house,
the lawn still unkempt,
the curtain perpetually
in need of replacement.

These days I only peek out
to see the bunnies
so at home
in our untended landscape,
as am I,
as am I.

Breaking News About Shoes

My hands, cupped and quivering
deliver this invitation to your inbox—

to pull your eyes from shiny screens
your kid's college acceptances
pictures of your firstborn's firstborn
canal views from your Venice trip.

It's not that those aren't pretty images—
glittered with your pride

but I'm waving to you from the sidelines,
listen well
and hear the miracle in my words—

she tried on shoes last Tuesday.
Two pairs!
In the store.
In the store!

I found the probable size
and we sat,
side by side
as I unlaced pink sneakers
until the mouth gaped wide enough.

One foot in, then the other,
and I tied.

She got up slowly,
trudged with me
up and down an aisle.

Are they tight?
Loose?
Rough?

Success was the NO
that slipped so smoothly from her lips,
butter on bread.

We repeated the process
untied another pair, gray this time.
Put feet in.
Tied
walked
talked again

Are you still with me?
Still here?

Last Tuesday
I have no pictures
but it's true, I swear,
(and I so rarely swear).

She tried on shoes,
we even bought a pair.

Her small smile told me
she was proud.

I was,
am still,
silly happy
to be a mom

whose daughter
tried on shoes
and chose a pair.

Your eyes have glazed over
I see your finger poised to delete

having never been
one who buys ten of everything,
sets a schedule—

*Let's try on one bra a day,
one pair of pants,
right shoe Monday
Tuesday left,*

Having never been the one
who has a Doctorate
in Making Returns.

Breaking news here from the front
which is usually the back
or side, where we are so invisible—
She tried on shoes
and even bought a pair.

Who Will Sing?

She gets older, this daughter of mine,
as do I, and the heavy question behind
each day, woven now into each year—
what about when I'm gone?

She can't live with you forever
I'm told, I know this to be true.
Some of her peers, twenty-ish,
thirty-ish, middle-aged,
have gone to group homes,
happily or not so.

Still the world spins.
More questions arise,
for the options aren't
pretty or plentiful,
and my imaginings vacillate
between dark and bleak.

Who will sing to her in the mornings,
and guard the rituals
that define her boundaries?

There are her questions
of songs, or objects, or days,
or other people, some of them dead,
some she has no contact with,

and I am to answer them
as if I am that person, that thing,
ten a week, typed up by Friday at 3 p.m.

There is the morning question or statement,
often cryptic, and she anxiously awaits
my videotaped response,
though I am in the same room.

There is the crucial, long-enough pause
between activities,
the deciphering of scrawled dreams,
decoding her language
in time to understand
she means This and not That,

planning the next day's snack,
next week's lunch,
offering my hair,
two-sided and girl-shaped,

reminding and re-answering
a hundred times a day,
why him and not her,
why people say this,
do that,

what it means to advocate
real-time with people,
rather than to the air,
in a corner, hours later?

You say—
she will adjust.
You say—
she will deal,
she'll learn to cope.

If I weren't so damned appropriate
I'd ask you what it would be like
if someone took control of you

because it's easier for them,
because they don't understand
what you need,
because there are four or five others
living with you who need things too.

What if the notes, the records,
the story of your life,
were left in a drawer unread, or read just once
by a supervisor
in an office somewhere.

What would it be like
if your clothes were too
rough against your skin,
and you didn't have the words?
Or, if you did,
they came out a month, a year later,
and so you had to wear these garments
that sandpapered your tender flesh
and then when you scratched
your arms until you bled,
what if you were given
a behavioral plan to curb
that thing you were doing to cope?

What would it be like
if the proverbial walls of your house,
the very things you count on

to be there, day after day,
your schedule, your calendar,
your To-Do list,
were erased one day?

What would it be like
if the people you count on—
let's call them staff—
changed every few months,
and didn't read the notes about you,
or forgot what was in them,

and you were expected to be compliant,
do as you're told,
even if you didn't like
the food you were given,
the activities you were driven to,
the staff you relied on
for food, a bath,
the others who shared the place
you are now supposed to call home?

Am I melodramatic, or just well-read?

You do the research,
go check out the houses
you say she should live in,
be the fly on the wall,
and then report back to me, please.

I distract myself
with the gifts, the burdens,
the details of her life.

Tea too hot,
song too rough,
packed lunch was uninteresting,
everything needs more salt.
In the land of autism
the tiniest thing
can make or break a day,

and when it breaks—
the day, or my heart—
the healing is slow, uneven,
and the memory of every assault
on the nervous system,
hers or mine,
seems imprinted on the walls
of her cells, of this place
she calls her home.

Here we incorporate it into the décor,
write poems about it,
scratch an itch against the rough
patch in the plaster.

We make it all right.

So, it's tell the truth time—
who will sing to her
when I'm gone?

Who will sing?

Smile

It was Tuesday,
six months and four days ago.
The incredible Dr. S
managed a first—
pedaling the chair back just a bit,
your face more accessible,
sunglasses shielding your eyes
from too-bright light.

He touched twenty dulled pearls
with his scaler,
probing slyly, quickly,
distracting with wide smiles,
silly faces, a joke
that floated far above
your comprehension.

Afterwards, the high fives and calm way-to-gos,
Let's do twenty-two next time.
My swells of gratitude
at the way they keep voices low,
avoid the balloon machine
in your presence,
mark progress in teeth "counted."

The next date carves itself
into your mind's firm clay
soon as your tuned ears hear
Yes, that Wednesday works,
11 am, only Dr. S, please—

and we were off,
out to lunch as promised,
basil eggplant and rice with soy sauce,
Mommy, I have your lemon please?

That evening he asked how it went,
this man who is more a father
than your own ever was,

and my mind goes to all those years
of terror and call-aheads—
*remember to have extra staff available,
three is best.
I'll bring my own bowl
because she always vomits,
and please,
no whirring machines, lights low,
don't even try to put metal in her mouth—*

and then I'm back here
with him, with you,
and we see something like
(could it be?)
pride lighting your round face
as you crow
*I did so well
at the tooth doctor.*

Bridges

We are pausing on a bridge
over the dwindling stream
that crawls through our local
dollop of green, Bird Park,

because we always pause, she and I,
on every little bridge
that spans any river anywhere,

so she can look down
from first one side,
then the other,
at that liquid light
which is water in the daytime,

one of many rituals
that string together our days
like a prayer flag.

I watch her watching water,
wondering if she notices
how much thinner the stream
than just last week.

My ear goes towards the toddler
tumbling in the grass nearby
which calls my gaze there, too.

The child laughs and spins
as her Mom or Aunt or Nanny
tosses a little pink ball
that quickly rolls into the stream.

Just as fast,
the child's laughter
turns to wails—
huge, garish sounds
from such a small body,

and my gaze shifts back to daughter,
who is now squinting,
covering her ears,
turning away from woeful child,
bridge and water,
and back towards the safety of the path.

She's now tense,
and each person, each dog we pass
might be a reason to become undone,
an insult to the tightly wound
system of nerves and cellular memories
ticking in linear, illogical time

and I think of all of us,
everywhere,
living with and without autism,
carrying years of triggers,
a hundred reasons to become undone,

and how we are each,
at any given hour, maybe
a few breaths away from meltdown.

The wonder is
how we hold it together,
or pretend to,
in a time when mass shootings
are just a few more ravages

punctuating the news cycle,
and everything seems cracked,
precarious.

We find the safety of the car,
and an hour later she
is singing luscious bluesy notes
in perfect pitch as she
peruses cookbooks

and my own triggers recede,
and I think *yes,*
this is how we go on.

Yes, this is how we'll go on.

Father's Day

On this day of all days
do you picture her sweet face,
and can you still hear
her laughter?

Do the cards and gifts
from your newer children
stir a longing in your heart,
or do they cover
the hole you dug long ago
when you excavated her from your life?

You should know she's amazing.
She sings
like an angel,
loves yellow ducks
all things pink,
and has grown taller than me.

Her autism does not define her.
Isn't the crime
your wife convinced you
was done to her, done to you.

She's not your litany
of complaints—
her lack of,
her refusal to,
her inabilities.

Whoever wrote *hell*
hath no fury
like a woman scorned
clearly meant mothers
who saw their children
scorned by their fathers.

Failure to parent,
failure to love,
failure to deserve a place
in her heart or mine.

On a good day,
I used to feel sorry for you.
On bad days, I was livid.

Lately, on better days—
I don't think of you at all.

Inheritance

You only caught glimpses
of your child
as he sped through toddlerhood
towards those labels
that mean everything
and nothing:
child, tween, teen, young adult.

Glimpses, you say,
as if it all tornadoed past you
while I stood stupefied,
hands in pockets,
by the side of some dusty cow path,
a perpetual look of dull
surprise on my unremarkable face.

Truth is,
over here our lives
are nothing like that.

My daughter and I have plodded along
like turtles in the too-hot sun,

pausing every few feet
to rest, to allow her
a few attempts at integrating
the latest sensory assault,

which could have been a wind
shaking the branches too fast,
or the distant sound
of a jake brake on a downhill semi
from a highway half a mile away.

Her needs are special,
which means our shimmy
is your slow dance,
our milestones
seem like simple addition
to your kid's calculus.

I'm used to it,
adept at appreciating
the kinds of beauty
that decorate this life
that chose me, and her.

It's not the pace of it all
that leaves me sweaty
and gasping for breath.

It's my head spinning
as other children date
and learn to drive,
go to college,
get married,
have babies,
buy a house,

flying so far from nests
their parents can't squint enough
to make out the tiny dot
their bodies make
as they soar onward,
commanding the skies.

Anxiety

I could take pictures
to post on Facebook,
showing the world
(or the twenty who'd read it)
my strongest *doing fine* face.

Maybe share
that one of me in the Florida sun,
beach behind, smiling into the iPhone
all shiny teeth
and *Aren't I lucky*
and *See how lovely it is here.*

Truth is,
this morning
my daughter woke
navigating a battlefield,
familiar and grim.

Her foes—
anxiety, obsessions,
compulsions—
filling her head
with demands and
little terrors,

and all I can do
is pierce my skin,
pull my heart through the hole,
weave my love into a soft armor
and drape it around her shoulders.

All I can do
from the periphery
is shoot blind bullets
into the invisibles
she wrestles,
use words
more powerful
than theirs,
hope to gain ground
through repetition.

All I can do
is turn myself
inside out,
reach into my center
to grab handfuls
of my fortitude

and toss them towards her,
Tell her *this is medicine,
this is relief,
this is salvation.*

Harmonious Discord

This morning I walked early,
mismatched garments
layered to repel a cold, spitting rain.

I'd pushed my husband's baseball cap
down hard over the knitted earband
I bought to share with my daughter,
one she rejected for not being soft enough,
or pink.

Featherweight Bean jacket
lifts me to frequent, silent praise
for its tireless rebuff
of even the most bitter winds—
its soft arms moving with mine.

This walking time—
tucked into the space
between my early rising
and her wake-up song,
before the gentle *time to get up*
directive I save for him—
has become sacred
in my other-centered life.

Rounding the first corner
of my favored route,
I looked down and laughed
One pink glove, hers,
one turquoise, mine.

and the shoes, laced with big gaps
between eyelets three and six
to nurture the well-worn feet

whose dorsal surfaces
are temperamental, and
wavy as the sea.

The thought and the smile
bubbled up together:
I am a walking exhibition
of my pieced-together life.

The daughter
with all her needs hanging out,
her talents slowly
coming to light
in explosions of art, word and song.

The man who adapted to both of us,
stepping in, a little
closer every year,
to father her.

The felines, who sleep tirelessly,
rising long enough
to eat and coat us with their fur—
black, white, gray and ginger.

Middle-aged me holds it all together
in multi-hued patches of love,
bits of colorful string,
a plush batting of hope.

An ode to harmonious discord
is not such a bad thing to be,

said I to self out walking.

What You Mean

I tell our story
at times from desperation
since you will surely outlive me.

The larger world ought to know
something of your shimmers—
the way you hear colors in every song,
can turn a pun deftly
without knowing the meaning of the words,
will readily recall, decades later,
the exact date
a person scolded you.

Sometimes, I write from untamed desire
to be generous with your innocence,
for every community seems fraught
with deception and guile.

The purity with which you see—
almost minimalist in its lack of gray areas—
would surely lighten, lift, and soothe.

One day is named a tall-haired boy,
which is bad.
Another day might be long-haired girl,
which is quite good indeed.

You are given a gift you don't like.
Why must you pretend you do?

You chose 5:15 for your dinner.
It's now 5:18.
Why is the dinner late?

At 1 p.m. he said
Be with you in a minute.
It's now 1:09.
Why shouldn't you get upset?

You have taught me,
among other things,
we cannot keep our eye
on any grand old flag,
nor do we peel our eyes
or keep them on a prize somewhere.
If we can hear
we cannot turn a deaf ear to anything.
A new chapter
means the next part of a book,
not a life.
Nobody has real butterflies
inside their stomachs.

Your questions
refresh with their honesty,
jostle assumptions,
make space for wonder.
And folks are hungry for wonder.

So I write
and share
asking along with you—
Why don't people say what they mean?

Letting Grow

When you were a fuzzy-headed
thing, with rings of flesh-like bracelets
around your wrists and ankles
I'd rock you into sleep,
alert to your slightest cry or sigh.

Near two decades later I hover
feeling out the distance.
How near, OK for you,
How far, tolerable for me.

Knowing you so intimately I could
map your body, birthmark to freckle to scar,
kyphotic and lordotic curves
of your spine.

It is so hard to let you go.

I release you in tiny increments,
handing you one decision at a time:
What will you wear today?
Biting my mama tongue
that wants to coo and cajole

It's cold out. It's January. What makes sense?

Learning painfully, in discrete trials,
to let you go singing
short-sleeved, cacophony of color,
plaid on stripe, into the snow.

Note: A *discrete trial* is a teaching tool within the framework of Applied Behavior Analysis, often used to help individuals with autism learn.

My Uncommon Daughter

My uncommon daughter
at twenty-three years,
is riddled with anxiety
and complicated fears.

Loose beads with holes
(they should be on a string!)
and thunder and lightning,
the power failure they may bring.

My uncommon daughter
moves mountains each day
just to get through the hours,
OCD in her way.

She struggles with things
many learn when quite young,
like shampoo, and showering,
and how clothing is hung.

My uncommon daughter
comprehends, then forgets
she clings to routine,
is indifferent to pets.

You may think her words nonsense—
she can be quite verbose
but you can glimpse patterns
if you listen, real close.

My uncommon daughter
has humor to share.
Her puns are quite nimble
literal and yet spare.

Her laugh is heard rarely
but oh when it flows
she bubbles with joy
from her nose to her toes.

My uncommon daughter
hears colors in song
she smiles when she's anxious
and we get it all wrong.

Though misunderstood,
she offers fresh perspective—
makes all of their judgments
seem so like invective.

My uncommon daughter
hasn't the least bit of care
what you think of her outfit
or how often you stare.

She gets so much right.
happy with simple things
prefers loose to tight—
no buttons or strings.

My uncommon daughter
is teaching me well
about patience, acceptance,
and how none can truly tell

what's inside the mind,
soul, and heart
of one labeled with autism
of one who stands apart.

This daughter, same as you
in the eyes of Creation,
is part of the rainbow
which is Autism Nation.

Comfort

It's not hard to tell you
how soft things
sing siren songs
to my abraded senses—

fleece sheets,
chenille sweaters,
the feel of my fingers deep
in my daughter's thick brown curls.

You understand
the implicit soothe
of mosses and eiderdowns,
so many sorts of velvet.

The flip side holds its own reward,
a calm that seems hopelessly
beyond explanation.

There's the shocking smack
of frigid air
slapping my cheeks—
nature's caffeine—
as I walk in winter dawn.

The way night diminishes gently
willing to extol the sun's arrival.

How gnawing hunger
elevates a simple cracker
to godliness.

Comfort needs
her inverse twin,
and I can't help but honor
them equally,

all that sublime illumination
like astral buttons
sewn into darkness.

Released

Each January rolled over and died,
left another set of miles
from that last time
you saw your daughter's face.

A man cannot be forced to be a father,
and perhaps your new children—
shiny and unblemished
by things like autism
and a likeness to a woman
you could not love—

filled the spaces in your heart,
or sucked up
all your scant reserves.

How could you
leave her in her bedroom all morning,
without breakfast,
didn't you realize she couldn't open the baby gate
that blocked her access to downstairs?

Why would you
repaint her pink bedroom to dull gray-brown
with no discussion, no warning?

How do you
live with yourself
30 minutes away
letting years pass without seeing her,
calling her?

I buried the questions,
let go the weighty layers
of grief and anger
marbled with disbelief.

Eight years and our daughter
had almost stopped
recounting all the times
you yelled at her,

repeating the cruel rules
your new wife had thrown
as if she could catch them,
as if she could comprehend
that which was foreign to her.

She'd almost stopped saying
don't want to see them,
don't make me go.

I never had to tell her
she wasn't welcome,
that you'd banned your firstborn
from your home.

Free, divorced from it all,
and then last week
my phone, your wife's name,
a voicemail I can neither
answer nor delete—

We are separated . . .
he doesn't live here now . . .
my children should know their sister . . .
do you want, do you want?

It's like bile rising
from a decade-old meal
and our daughter says *no,*
don't want to.

I echo her words in my mind,
willing my feet to step
around the sludge
dumped yet again
in my path.

Keep moving,
keep breathing,
keep looking forward.

Say a prayer
for the frayed bond,
between father and daughter
then let it go.

Grocery Shopping
May 2020

We take ourselves to the market—
me in run-of-the-mill layers
of self-consciousness—
quick glance in rearview,
hand rising to smooth the hair,

she baring all, as usual—
jacket askew, short curls untamed—
no pretense, nothing to hide.

Our market rule
in the time of virus:
*No touching anything, honey,
except yourself or Mom.*

We've gotten good at this,
practicing since mid-March,

and so we go,
in service to our shopping list
following the one-way arrows
like breadcrumbs.

Her singing beams
a Disney-flavored sunshine
up and down the aisles
even through her mask.

She pauses in front of the dairy section,
halts her sun-beaming mid-note
and announces to the floor,
Mommy, it looks like I have to pee.

No beats to skip—
we're well prepared,
the purple handled pee jug
ready in the backpack,

nestling up against
the toilet paper,
flanked by two packs
of antiseptic wipes.

Into the bathroom we go—
I shoulder doors, find a stall,
hook the pack, and pull out

the magnificent portable
receiver of pee
that makes all outings
possible, conquerable.

My thought-out plan
for safety and practicality
backlit by the simplicity
of her needs,
which aren't so much *special*
as they are honest,

the whole thing shined up
by my gratitude, in recent years,
that she can name the sensations,
usually in time to stay dry.

We're engaged
in familiar activities:
she's peeing
and I'm silently marveling
at what the world could be
if we were all more like her—

free of innuendo, honest to a fault,
unable to fathom tap dancing
to any music but our own.

The Life Cycle of a Day

On a Massachusetts March afternoon,
still scarved and gloved, we drive

quiet back roads—harder to find
as new neighborhoods overtake old forest,

and she is almost silent—
a rare thing in our universe.

The Audubon sanctuary
welcomes us with a near empty lot

sweet relief to we
who struggle with traffic and crowds.

She does her bathroom trip
before we ramble along a familiar loop,

the windless woods still,
fields dun-colored, dry.

A sturdy boardwalk hovers
above sleepy waters,

winding a storybook path
through the red-maple swamp.

It floods sometimes, dark liquid
pushing up through the slats

so our boots make music as we step
carefully, to keep pants dry.

We trust the boards over quiet wetlands
that seem to be dozing

until I spot three white masses softly anchored
around submerged branches, their warty shine enticing.

We lean in, close enough to see
black dots clinging together

inside little jelly globes like individual solar systems
punctuating the orange-black waters.
I default to words where none are necessary—
her quiescence tells me no questions have surfaced.

I say egg, *tadpoles, the gradual transformations
that turn one-eyed drops of jelly into frogs.*

A short silence, and then she says
Marine means ocean animals. Salty water.

Yes I say and we walk on,
equally delighted with our watery connections,

she in her own sea of images,
me breathing in scents of mud, spring, a fleeting peace.

Unbroken

There were times
I imagined you different.

My young-mother mind
pictured you—
normal, typical, non-disabled.

I can't use those words anymore
for their opposites evoke—
lack, absence, tragedy,

and you, my child,
are a celebration of plenty,
a bounty of delight,
a well of fascination.

In fact, you stand against the backdrop
of pedestrian life
in sharp relief
adding color where there is none.

I looked up the opposite of disabled—
unaffected, activated, unbroken.

At 29, you appear much younger
and I wonder how typicality
would have changed you.

Plucked eyebrows,
black eyeliner,
a flat iron to tame
your wild dark chocolate curls?

You might have dieted,
finding fault with your shape and size,
and worn heels that hurt your tender feet.

You would not go singing
through the grocery store
happily oblivious to strange looks.

Typical you
may not have sung at all,
thinking a note or two
off-key.

There are many times
I imagine the world
different than it is,
a welcoming place
where compassion and respect are the norms,

and we all go singing
through the aisles.

Longing
Mothering my autistic child during Covid

Longing
to help you know
in your bones, child,
in your bones,
this will pass.

This will pass
and I'm longing
for you to know
we will again be free
to dip in and out
of those beloved scrawls
on your wall calendar—

horse riding and art class,
the candy and craft stores,
restaurants,
swimming at the Y,
and your weekly volunteer job
tidying the bins at the toy store,
pricing stuffed animals.

You will once again
return to your day program
where you may even welcome
those groups you do not love—
news and movie talk
trivia and talent show.

I know in my bones,
which are just older versions
of your own,
that this will pass.

All things do,
and we will re-rise,
rise again, grateful
and eager to push forth
into the too-loud world
carrying earplugs
and fidget toys,
your soft pink ball of yarn.

Until then, my frightened
full-grown child,
I will be here,
to answer your questions,
daily, hourly.

No, this won't for last 100 days.
No, this won't be for your whole life.

Yes, we'll go out walking
today and tomorrow and every day.

No, this won't be forever,
No, I don't know the day,
the hour, it will end.

Yes, the power will stay on.
Yes, you'll swim in the ocean
come summer.

This will pass.
I'm longing
to help you know
this will end.

Salt

She began this way—
floating in amniotic waters,
bobbing in the waves
my movements made
already ingesting salty fluid
like the ocean she'd grow to love
all of her years.

Sweat
from fever and exertions.
Tears
from joy and misery—
both reduce to crystals
that remind her of inlet immersions,
awaken her curious tongue.

Why we can't drink ocean water?
Why we can only have a little?
She asks over and over.

I am ever ready
with the right answers—

It's not good for us.
Our bodies need fresh
water fresh water fresh . . .

But why
she asks
as if for the first time—
why I can't drink the ocean
drink the sea why

it's ok for swimming but not
to swallow too much
why only a little
why mommy why mommy why . . .

My answers, perfectly formed,
like my ready retorts
to all her repetitive questions

because because because

You already salt everything.
Your muscles get thirsty
without clear, fresh drinks.

Bodies need more
than just candy and desserts
bodies need sleep,
fruits and vegetables,
good protein
fresh water fresh air fresh . . .

On the thirtieth anniversary
of becoming her mother,
or rather when she
stayed a wondrous five years old
in a grown-up body,

I remembered when she was a fish
rolling in my internal ocean.
Somersaults, hiccups,
at ease in my briny stew.

More relaxed than she nearly ever
is in her separate body
in a world that refuses to make sense.

I wanted to say then,
want to say now—

Drink, Honey, drink.
Take in all the ocean you desire.
Let it soothe and calm you.
Let it ease your way.

Who am I to tell you
what or when or how?
Who am I
except your welcoming harbor
in a sea of endless storms?

I Must Want This

The weight of caregiving.
The way she is perpetually a child.

Shouldering her care
year after aging year,

I carry periorbital shadows
deepening under eyes that peer
back from every mirror,

casually studying
the channels
engraved across my forehead,

flesh under chin sagging
in silent protest against worry.

Perhaps it's my dharma
that I plod through the cycles—
dawn to dusk,
week to month,
winter dripping into spring,
summer crisping into fall
and back again—

awakening her gently,
the pre-breakfast dream recap,

Let's match our clothes to the weather;
shorts for summer, sweatshirts for November,

*Let's find the pretzels, the water bottle,
close the soup lid tight.*

The daily details—
*What will the snack be?
Where will we go this afternoon?
What's for dinner?*

Strategies to tame anxiety:
verbal checklists,
ball of soft yarn to hold,
deep breaths,
ask for space,
advocate, advocate, advocate.

Yes, you can get through it.

Evenings, on stiffening knees I bend
to wash her hair, cut her toenails,

and last night,
with flashlight pointed
at her private areas,
I looked for any source
for the "pee ouch"
and "poop hurts,"

grateful because she could name
her discomfort,
and it's possible whereabouts,

because I do love growth,
will gladly take it
in any form,
any hour, day or night.

I must have asked for this—
the alternative universe
of perpetual caregiving,
my only child
always a child,

my never empty nest
a little bare,
holes showing daylight,
straw droopy in places,

a bit worn out to carry
all the need
because nests were never
meant to last this long.

What Not to Do When Decluttering

Three bags stood
at the ready,
blue marker proclaiming them—
Keep, Toss, Donate.

William Morris said it best—
anything that stays must prove its worth
or dazzle with its beauty.

I coaxed the jaws
of her closet open,
my honeyed hum
companion to fervent,
ever-fresh intention.

A midnight blue hatbox
with fading gold stars
marching across its top
called from behind a jumble
of her winter boots

and downed t-shirts—
all larger than my own now—
pinned under a fallen hanger.

The frayed lid lifted easily
revealing a clutch of photographs gone sticky
through too many summers
and general neglect.

Aloud to myself: *Yup. These can go.*

Poking out from under
this priceless, useless mash,
a field of tiny fuschia daisies
freckling some still-soft cotton.

I fingered a sleeve the length of my hand,
lifted the whole of it tenderly
into the bright October light.
Tiny legs flapped from the motion.

Once-white collar stiff to my touch,
lace gone yellow with years
and old spit-up stains.

Next moment I was lifting her
from the plastic car seat
with its cheery balloon cushion,
my breath paused
to protect her sleep.

My sagging breasts tingled,
as if her hunger needed quelling,
her lamb-like cry needed quieting,
even though she lay heavy in sleep
on my shoulder.

Outside the window
a mail truck rumbled by,
snapping me back
into presence—October afternoon.

What could I do, then,
but gather the babywear
to my face,
bury my nose deep
into the field of flowers?

As my creased cheeks
grew damp
and the soft cotton
became handkerchief

what could I do
but anoint its utility,
fold it tenderly,
name it
Keep, Keep, Keep?

Emergency

A typical Tuesday morning.
Three adults—
daughter, husband, self.

I'm the whirling dervish.
Care for the cats, feed the dishwasher,
wipe down that counter full of crumbs.

He preps his tea, she her breakfast
following the steps we've practiced
for the last two months.

Get cup and juice,
pour it three quarters full.
Open freezer, find the bag
of individually wrapped cornbread.

Small plate—
second shelf, cabinet next to stove.
Unwrap one golden square,
retrieve butter from refrigerated cubby.

Deposit the cornbread on its ivory throne
crown with a pat of salted sunshine.

Microwave on Defrost 1.

At the beep, she opens
the microwave door,
announces
Mommy, the plate is broken.

My pride flashes
It's not yet old—
this ability she's developing
to communicate such a thing.

Slipping in between daughter
and curiously severed plate,
I retrieve the pieces,
the crumbly square,
throw them away.

We'll need to start over
I say,
*What would you do
if you were by yourself?*

Tell you or him.

What if we were not here?

Not skipping a beat,
this child in a woman's body,
confidently says

Call 911.

The Truth About My Slow

Life with my child,
my adult child,
has not been an easy one.

Oh, the trials I could essay
into and poem against!

Stories to make you sad
for me, for her,
for the world we all co-create.

Stories of doctors,
specialists, therapists,
teachers, family
and other moms
finding her flaws,
suggesting my
parenting may not be
the best way forward.

Stories of her father
who has not seen her
in well over nine years
because she flushed
an empty toothpaste tube
down his toilet
bursting his pipes.

His ceiling leaked
all over his young
wife and their shiny
new children and,
well, they can't have that.

But I didn't pick up
this leaky pen
to wax miserable
about life
with a special needs kid
who is now an adult.

My child,
fascinating
and intense
and curious,
is part
of what has saved me.

We take it slow,
she and I,
and our he who joined us later.

We take it way down.
Try ten notches.

She was 6 when toilet
replaced two identical potties.
('Til then I had to carry one everywhere
In a giant green plastic trash bag.)

At 25 she was finally able to tell me
of the abuse she suffered
from a teacher when she was 9. 10.

Happy, on any afternoon,
with a nature walk,

she sings to the wind
with child-like joy
between the repetitive questions *du jour*—
Why so-and-so said such and such?
Why other girls won't have girl hair?
Why we can't go back to Kindergarten?

30, she prepares her own breakfast—
This after lists of directions
and many trials.
When the food choices change,
we begin all over again.

We have created
our own way
into walking and talking
into answers
and lessons
about self-advocacy.

We are finding
our own path
along the meandering stream,
around the park,

pausing often to take in
the leaves swimming
against a windy current.

Have you noticed
just how extraordinary they are?

Perpetuum

This caregiving life
became a marathon
around year twenty.

To manage every detail of a life—
not my own, but equally precious—
required stamina, focus and grit.
(And still does.)

My energy waned
even as enthusiasm
retained youthful contours.

Thirty years in,
I note further incursions of angst
keeping pace with drooping skin,
worn joints and thinned patience.
The mirror informs me drily
that it's triathlon now.

Keep running keep swimming
keep those legs pumping
her well-being depends on this.

I love her more than I can write,
would dig all the way,
as they used to say,
to China—with my hands!
if it were fueled by heart alone.

There are days, though,
when digging deeper
doesn't seem possible.

When I don't believe I can
face another dozen rounds
of repetitive questions,

offer my graying hair
for a tenth sensory soothe,
or bend to shave her legs
again. Again.

There are weeks I scan faces
of people driving by me,
or wheeling their shopping cart
in the opposite direction

looking for signs
there might be someone
who could step in someday.

Kind eyes, open hearts—
anything that will quell
the voices in my head
that whisper, chide, rasp—

Who will do it all
with enough grace
and love
and utmost care
when I'm gone
when I'm gone?

Waiting

It's a torture,
unseen flies that bite her tender ankles,
the scree of fingernails making S shapes
on a wall of chalkboard paint.

When? When? Exactly when

will the ride arrive
the snack be ready
the weather turn
from sweatshirt
to shorts?

Wait
isn't a *definitely*.
It's not a *yes, for sure,*
you can count on it.

When a person can thrive
only in houses made of rules,
uncertainty is hurricane,
tornado, blowing all things precious
out into the gaping night.

She loves sure-itude
which may not be a word.
Her truth doesn't reside in dictionaries

but dwells in the linear—
calendars, clocks, weather charts—
the vault of photographic memory.

Anxiety roots in those gaps
between expected and actual.
She wants a life on time,
with seamless schedules—
such sweet, paradoxical freedom.

My Calling

My revolution is a quiet one.
It stems from seeds planted by spirit
before I was born.
Its leaves sprout
only with the good rain of compassion
that sometimes tastes like tears. It blooms
only in the rich, common human soil,
the ground trodden and tilled by millions of sisters
and brothers with one heart beating
in its own time, just like mine.
Just like me.

My struggle is a flexed muscle,
so small and slow it's easy not to see it.
My fight is not a fight,
rather a realized intention
to shut up
and listen with the ears of my heart—
a waiting garden—

so I might then sing and chant
and poem exhortations,
urge others to quiet and still
so they may hear truth.

Listen, listen—
Love hums in time with heartbeats,
we are one we are one we are one.
What we do to each other,
we do to ourselves.
What we visit upon ourselves
we foist on others. Let it be worthy.

When I am all used up
and my bag of gifts is empty,
when my body gives itself
to the fire or to the earth,
when my small voice becomes
an integral part of the great OM
which is the song the Earth
hums as she spins through space,
my *peace* will be revolutionary.

Post script let them say
She did what she came here to do,
what it was she was called to,
what she was called for,
what she was called to be,
and though it was tiny
it was her own kind of mighty,
her own kind of vital
her own kind of fierce.

Dear Future Roadmaker
for the parent of the recently diagnosed

I promise
this will pass.
Not the diagnosis, of course,
or your cellular memories
of initial shock, sadness, despair.

But this crisis—
the one that's shredded
your equanimity,
kept you up some nights
for months,

that involves biting
and teachers,
veiled threats
from Those-Who-Decide
your son may not be appropriate
for their coveted program,

the lauded school
that took
five meetings,
twelve months,
most of your energy
and an attorney
to finally welcome him
into their fold—

it will pass.

Your current devastations—
Johnny rides the short bus.
There will be no prom or diploma,
no college, career, or wedding—
these things will fade
into insignificance.
Give it time.

And besides
short bus = fewer students,
fewer stops, less sensory overload,
and sometimes, a kinder driver.

There are special proms,
if he is so inclined,
and certificates
of completion, now.

Take a breath.
Safeguard your energy.
You will need
every precious bit.

Choose your battles,
don't try to war
in many places
at once,

and know this:
I am here.
There are many of us,
veterans who stepped
into the forest's dark
growth and trod
the faint paths left
by those who came before us,
and we are making roads of them.

Don't underestimate yourself
or your son.

You will both grow callouses,
know such triumphs,
and despairs you fear
will wreck you.

They won't.
You will emerge tougher,
a warrior advocate.
All the roadmakers
will be there cheering

and someday
that documented
list of deficits,
all his can'ts
and won'ts
will cease to faze you.

Mama lion,
future road maker,
mark my fervent words,

your child,
son of your heart,
will surprise you with his gains,
amaze you with his resilience,
delight you with his awareness,
and make you
very,
very
proud.

About the Author

Melinda Coppola penned her first poem—about the color pink—at the tender age of 8. Her relationship with writing was mercurial for decades, but once she learned that her blood type is, in fact, *poet*, she settled into a kind of quiet cohabitation with her muses.

Melinda's poetry has been nominated for Best of the Net and received The Reader's Choice Award (Songs of Eretz Poetry Journal). Her work has appeared in *Thimble Literary Magazine, One Art by A Journal of Poetry, Willows Wept Review, Press 53, Mutha Magazine, Last Stanza Poetry Journal, Chicken Soup for the Soul: Raising Kids on the Autism Spectrum,* and *Amethyst Review,* among others. This is her first full-length poetry book. After 10 + years of gestation and labor, she is profoundly grateful that her "work of heart" has finally been born.

In addition to writing poetry, she paints, communes with stones on Cape Cod beaches, and teaches Yogabilities™, her own approach to Yoga for individuals with special needs. She lives in Massachusetts with her husband, her daughter, and a small herd of cats.

Visit her online at
melindacoppola.com

www.ingramcontent.com/pod-product-compliance
Lightning Source LLC
Chambersburg PA
CBHW072155160426
43197CB00012B/2397